A Wide Eyes Publishing

Anthology

www.wide-eyes-publishing.com

publishing people who want to raise hell with their truths.

ISBN-13: 978-1-7339013-3-8

War Crimes Against the Uterus

poems of resistance

Contents

Letters from the editors...

The work in this anthology is truly a preservation of history — these poems, reactions, and confessions encapsulate the complete disregard for reproductive rights and bodily autonomy in the United States. More importantly, these words come from a place of pain and experience. Each piece has delved deep into the lives of writers and has allowed them to come from a place of truth – which is just the spark of this revolutionary work. Their call to action is a beacon for all of us to listen to and stand for. This has been a 200-year fight for reproductive rights. A 200-year fight for *autonomy over our own fucking bodies. For freedom of CHOICE.* Enough is enough. With this book and these words, we ask you to leave this at the doorstep of your legislators, educators, and senators. Send it to the White House. Send it to your parents, your pro-life neighbor, or your friend who just had an abortion. When this is released, this will be used as a tool – because these are our stories, this is our reality, and these are our god damn bodies.

This is a scary and pivotal moment in history, and the truth deserves to be preserved – by a source that honors the sanctity of those who are brave enough to share their own. We are not in the business of covering up, directing, or altering these stories in order to fit our own narrative; we are in the business in letting these poems and poets speak for themselves. May their work raise hell, spread brutal truth, and cultivate change.

Jean-Marie Bub, Editor in Chief, Founder Wide Eyes Publishing

It's been a privilege and an honor being able to work with these people, these poems, and for this purpose. It's been an incredible experience reading these stories and having a physical manifestation of a movement so powerful is so needed right now. This book is the embodiment of publishing people who are raising hell with their truths, and I hope you find power in these words as we have.

Kayt Christensen, co-Editor, Author "Inevitable Ignition"

To every writer who submitted their stories... THANK YOU.

Thank you for bravely expressing yourself in such a raw, honest, and open way. If you follow me on any platforms you know that I am passionate about raw self-expression where we don't censor ourselves for any reason. And as writers, we all know that's harder to do than to theorize about. There is nothing more important in this life than expressing ourselves in whatever medium aligns with us. You all have expressed yourself so honestly and openly and you amaze me. Please know that doing this work gives space and courage to others to safely and honestly express themselves without fear. The topics in this anthology are not simple and not easy to read about, write about, and most importantly, to experience. You all are some fearless, badass, magical human beings!!! Your stories matter. No matter what anyone says, or how many people it feels aren't listening... Your. Stories. Matter. Your voices matter. Period.

The work that goes into being a writer can be overlooked by many, and one reason I value Wide Eyes so much is that in this space you are HEARD and safely held by the people who are housing your work. This anthology is full of stories that will be hard to read for some, and for some, your stories are going to benefit for the rest of time and allow them the room and courage to tell their own stories. Thank you for being so courageous, so open, and so trusting of Jean, Kayt, Sophia, and I as your editors. This is an important time to speak up. Be proud of yourselves for doing so. We have so much love for you all.

Samantha Rose Johnson, co-Edtior, Founder Pussy Magic

Jean called me from the other side of the world, first thing in the morning, to pitch this anthology to me. It was a mere two days after the Heartbeat Bill had sent shock waves across the United States, and caused a ripple effect throughout the entire world. Needless to say, I jumped at the offer.

Our uteruses are no strangers to oppression. They have been betrayed by those we trusted, invaded by those unwelcome, and stripped of their rights by those who have no right. This anthology is for the ones who stand in solidarity. Who aren't afraid to face up to the patriarchy. Who value their voices and the stories they tell.

Thank you for sharing all of your raw, emotionally-charged, painful, poignant and heart-wrenching journeys. Thank you for your transparency. Thank you for trusting us with your hearts - and uteruses.

Sophia Mihailidis, co-Editor, co-Founder Womxn Rising

trigger warning:

these works contain highly in-depth descriptions about abortion, abuse, sexual assault, rape, incest, self-harm, and more.

Throughout the book, I've included facts for educational purposes. For some, these facts may be considered triggering.

Please do not hesitate to reach out for help. See our resources on the next page if you need someone to talk to, are feeling anxious, or feel depressed.

Resources

National Alliance on Mental Illness (NAMI).....1-800-950-NAMI

Substance Abuse and Mental Health Services Administration
(SAMHSA)...800-662-HELP

Crisis Text Line: Text CONNECT to 741741

National Suicide Prevention Lifeline...............1-800-273-TALK

For unbiased information about abortion and about other
resources, including financial assistance............ 1-800-772-9100
(National Abortion Federation)

this is how revolutions begin.

untitled
by Jean-Marie Bub
   previously published in "Reclaim: An Anthology of Women's Poetry"

if the pain
that a woman bares
is far too
foreign
for your comprehension,

then you shall have
no say
in what happens
to her womb.
her bleeding body
is not your battleground,

and there is no debate —
she who harbors humanity
should control her own fate.

The Match That Set the House On Fire
by Emily Perkovich

I FEEL THE GHOST OF EVERY HAND THAT WAS EVER
SWATTED AWAY.

I FEEL EVERY FINGER
THAT CRAWLED INSIDE ME
FEIGNING MISUNDERSTANDING.
I FEEL MYSELF FULL WITH WHAT I DID NOT ASK FOR.

FULL WITH DISAGREEMENT,
POURING OUT MY BLOODIED, RAW THROAT.
FULL WITH THE WORDS PINNING ME DOWN.

AND FULL WITH FIRE AT THE REALIZATION THAT THERE
WAS TRUTH NAUGHT BEHIND THE WORDS.

FULL WITH FIRE, BRIMMING OVER.
FULL WITH FIRE, POOLING BETWEEN MY LEGS.
FLAMES LICKING MY THIGHS.
LASHING IN HOT BREATHS
AT EACH HAND THAT DARES
AFTER BEING SWATTED.
WHIPPING AND SCORCHING
THE CREEPING FINGER TIPS.
ENVELOPING ME FULL.

AND BURNING THE WORDS AWAY INTO CHARRED RUINS.

AND THE GHOSTS DO NOT LEAVE.
I CARRY THEM WITH ME.
BUT I NO LONGER CARRY THE BLAME.

THAT
BELONGS TO YOU.

AND YOU SPARKED AN INFERNO WHEN YOU TRIED TO
PLACE IT INSIDE OF ME.

WELCOME TO YOUR PRIVATE BONFIRE.

TONIGHT
FOR ONCE,
WE WILL BURN
you
AT THE STAKE.

2019 "Heartbeat Bill" Exposes Cowboys by Tyler Zeanah

the judicial system is tossing my uterus
around in the air, cowboy lasso
swinging with genocide and the curdled
war cries of history repeating. men disguised
as teenage boys riding the world
horseback into their locker room club
full of jock talk with a stolen pair of panties
from someone's little sister.
my cervix is fixed in a vice on the
stand but she can't speak up
with all the white man's hands
shoving religion down my forcibly
unbuttoned pants, "what a pretty,
little thing you are, sweetheart.
all the more perfect to bleed for me,
my seed, and what you don't want done
in the name of your body.
but i hold dominion over you in the name
of the father, the son, and the holy spirit
so come here babygirl, amen."
the government would rather stare down
my shirt searching for their expired God

than face their mother's wailing in the truest
betrayal of hellfire for what they've done to her.

Banning and criminalizing abortion doesn't put an end to abortions, it just puts lives in danger.

"Preventing women and girls from accessing an abortion does not mean they stop needing one. That's why attempts to ban or restrict abortions do nothing to reduce the number of abortions, it only forces people to seek out unsafe abortions."

Read it for yourself...

https://www.amnesty.org/en/what-we-do/sexual-and-reproductive-rights/abortion-facts/

The best form of flattery, the right form of flattery, the white form of flattery
by Mikhayla Robinson

White women

Come up to me
And tell me
How much they admire my tresses,

Wishing their hair would act as mine does...

But when it comes to living a black girl life,
When it comes to living *at all* while black,
They are silent.

Black girl magic to them
Is a D
     I
       S
         A
           P
            P
              E
              A
            R
           I
       N
    G

Act,
Taking away all of the struggle,
While only keeping the "palatable" parts.

Admiration,
White woman to black woman,
Comes at the price of life.
In other words..

YA'LL LIKE MY HAIR,
YA'LL LIKE MY LIPS,
YA'LL LIKE EVERYTHING ABOUT ME,
BUT DON'T CARE ABOUT MY LIFE,
MY HEALTH,
MY LIFE.

What about Us
by Sarah M. Crowder

Do you not see the sons and daughters fighting to live now,
Have you forgotten them,
Forsaken their very existence,
Let's worry about our children in the streets,
The children in foster homes,
Waiting for someone to love them,
When there is not enough love to give,
Let's worry about the ones who have waited on us first,
Then worry about limiting women's rights,
When we have our priorities straight.

Faustian Straw Man
by Jolene Bresney

There's a burning in my belly, a sickness with blades that sharpen
themselves on my racing thoughts coiling around conflicting
confusion
Understanding is coming loose,
'standing' is crumbling, all I feel is 'under' in my hope.
An oppression that's winding back the hands of years to a time where
breath brimmed
with desperation nailed to war-torn bodies
Disguised as concern that can't prove itself,
a thief that reeks of an insidious agenda that makes choice a crime,
and crime is a two-
prong life sentence carrying trauma with a heartbeat and ordained
suffering
Born headfirst into a corrupt world that values nothing more than a
first breath ghosted
by compassion at a fleshy point of entry
A land that kneels to weapons with a mouth full of bullets and a flag
that's lost it's
meaning
A women's body repeating the destiny of unraveling in alleys with
death graffitied on
the walls turning hands into bloodstained sorrow
I can pretend this is about valuing life, but history is lodged in my
throat and I choke on
the hollow words of a single-minded reasoning wearing the name of
religion in a
secular society
My eyes can't erase the graves of school shootings, greedy wars, and
traffic stops

warped into justified casualties — the land of the free is an American
pipe dream, rusting
in its crimes
Violence is a sanctioned creed, deprivation is a deserved suffering we
close our eyes to,
erasing compassion we can laugh at with pointed fingers,
casting blame on the weak
Finding fault in faults that wear injury in their bloodstream
The truth is death will always be death wearing different shapes,
denial can't escape
bruised endings
The worse sentence is a life bound to apathy, rights are extended to
seeds and not the
living suffering forced to swallow their needs in thoughts and prayers
corroding the
tongue
I walk back to a stilled memory of a college roommate impregnated
by her grandfather
in secret. The pain moves through veins in slow motion. A choice she
didn't choose
that's a gift of a silent crime,
it's the seed of an evil entry
The body can become a home to a horror the heart will hold and
break in the teeth of
broken dreams
Say this disgusts you, you can't scrub the filth of these words from
your eyes
This ending of innocence ended in an rightful ending.
Wrongs deserve the saint of exile to a window of freedom without
judgment — a hurt
that never sleeps with the corrosion of prosperity

You can plant your beliefs in your skin, but you can't smother them in
faces of those
who have crime tattooed on their bodies
Whose bones rattle with screams of violation that can't hear prayers
in the memory of
their suffering
Deserving a choice of a future that has the right to a life without a
living reminder of a
crime they didn't choose.

False Ownership
by Megha Sood

This is strangely annoying.
when you see arrogance in
someone who doesn't own a thing
Can't conjure a thing out of thin air
let alone a human being.

You are just the renter here. You don't own shit.
you are born from this womb
which cradles your existence for months
a sliver away from called a being

Nothing but a pulsating existence in a foreign body
Sometimes the body treats it like an infection
to keep away the contamination
self-purging, an act of reclamation

Sometimes it accepts
cups its own palm
supports you, carries it to term
Its the body,
the arrangement
the unsaid understanding
a solemn promise
between the body and its identity

Your existence is slowly molded

like a ball of sagging clay on the potter wheel
morphed and molded
to be called a human being

You don't own the womb.
You definitely don't own our bodies.
You break the arrangement
just like to possess the things
Let me clear this
for the sake of your understanding
the body is not for your taking
There is a thin line between
The choices we make and your wanting.

Women aren't the only people who need access to abortions.

"…intersex people, transgender men and boys, and people with other gender identities who have the reproductive capacity to become pregnant.

One of the foremost barriers to abortion access for these individuals and groups is lack of access to healthcare. Additionally, for those who do have access to healthcare, they may face stigma and biased views in the provision of healthcare, as well as presumptions that they do not need access to contraception and abortion-related information and services. In some contexts, 28% transgender and gender non-conforming individuals report facing harassment in medical settings, and 19% report being refused medical care altogether due to their transgender status, with even higher numbers among communities of color."

Read it for yourself...

https://www.amnesty.org/en/what-we-do/sexual-and-reproductive-rights/abortion-facts/

I Am Not Her Bones
by T.J. McGowan

I am not her bones.

I am not in the miles walked carrying ghosts

and nightmares from roads I can't travel.

I am not behind her eyes or in the synapse spark

that flashes with stark memory of darker days.

I am much too quiet.

Closed lips are a wall in the way

and I'm so sick and tired of always choosing

to have nothing to say.

Look, if you want Gilead

pick up a fucking book,

stick to the fiction.

Keep your convictions from convicting

women conflicted with a choice we'll never have to make,

and, fellas, every word not spoken

is a word we've stolen

from a step forward

another voice is trying to take.

Place a stake in unity,

dust the rust of your tongues

and do more than the minimal due diligence

before distorted views of God and religion

control decisions

over the very sacred thing

that keeps us from becoming completely invisible,

the autonomy over our bodies as individuals.

As men, our insides will never be treated like territory up for grabs

or some unlawful land requiring regulation,

because its anatomy is the key to humanity.

And, I say key, because at the core

of my beliefs, I believe

the power of life should be left in the hands

of the bodies that can unlock its door.

They try to say this is God's ways,

last I checked this isn't a Theocracy,

as broken as we may be, we are still meant to be a Democracy,

the hypocrisy hidden behind this bible-bound mockery

putting stock in beliefs blended with governance

to govern over flesh and womb, entombing women,

as if believing your blessed makes you better than the rest.

Preaching and reaching with words I've never seen

in the teachings of Jesus, and this piece is

not a knock against you if you've got faith, that's great,

as long as it breeds peace and compassion,

and to those who passionately oppose abortion,

I get that you have the right to protest and light your torches,

force it on followers in a place of worship until you are blue in the

face,

but the nerve to think you can create law,

makes you a day late and a dollar short.

I've got a penny for your thoughts

if you can explain to me, how you claim to be – American,

and at the same time constantly contort your brain to see

around the separation of church and state.

Knelt in prayer and war ready,

steadily aimed at creating a criminal

out of free will,

trivializing half of human existence,

while screaming the only freedom restricted

is that which limits the itch in some trigger finger thrill

in case they're deemed unfit to equip themselves

with something meant to kill.

Politicians propositioned and propped up to pass legislation

in favor of pompous pontiffs and hollow prophets

using false pretense to convince ignorance into swallowing women

whole,

soulless and so full of hatred to think it okay

that women deserve to serve a longer sentence

than the men that rape them.

And who the fuck are they kidding

when they claim to give a shit about our kids.

To believe that is to be a fool,

as they force motherhood on little girls,

pushing babies into a world

where they'll only live long enough

to be shot at their school.

Speaking of education,

they want to drain dollars from resources,

placing weapons on teachers

with no raise in pay,

while reinforcing the hallways

with ways to imprison the youth.

A child's truth is fear now

and it's clear how

after birth

their worth is weightless

as they wade through the blood of friends funerals,

reading eulogies in replace of books.

Look, if you want to try and make it illegal to be a woman,

I better see you out there adopting those babies,

protesting for the ones in cages,

fighting to lower the costs of medication,

and aiding in raising form the cup you've forced to runneth o'er.

Woven into the fabric of time will not be their crimes,

but those that strip assistance, sitting on high horses,

ripping away provisions, limiting access to contraception,

a complete deception that they're pro-life.

If an unborn child is a gift, than why

after the Mother is dry-eyed and sutured

do they not give a fuck about her future?

They rather soon forget it and I get it,

once present this "present" is no longer something new,

no longer a self-righteous excuse,

no longer and extension or tool they use

in an unending fight to crucify those they refuse

to see, as anything more than sinners,

forgetting, the crucifix they grip

is adorned with the idea of forgiveness,

no longer a way to generate millions

to fix the vote for geriatric pricks

dictating laws with their dicks,

ignoring the fact that all they've done

is seal the fate of their own crucifixion.

Look, as I've said, I am not her bones.

I am also not her at home, alone,

with tough collision of heart and mind.

I am not her thoughts or body,

but my silence sure-as-shit

has contributed to her hard times.

I am not able to fully understand her pain,

but human rights violations are not something we should ever need

explained,

and I know you see it, too, so fellas, let me ask you,

to please reconsider sitting on the sidelines like I regretfully used to.

Freedom From Choice
by Alicia Young

Duped by power hungry wolves
in custom suits
and black robes
striking conservative gavels
Swindled by snake oil salesman
preaching righteousness from pulpits built with political payola
Testosterone filled narcissists
with a God complex
who sat in silence while children were stolen
from their mothers claim dominion over wombs
giving no choice to families
forcing frightened victims of violence
and trauma underground
It's time to replace complacency with roars
and fight to maintain what is taken for granted
because today it's choice
tomorrow speech
and eventually
freedom

I Just Wanted To See My Sunshine
by Gabrielle Caudle-Williams

Women have several things to hear about pregnancy

"We're sorry for your loss"

"Congratulations!"

"We can't find a heartbeat."

"What will you name the baby?"

"When's the funeral?"

"Is it a boy or a girl?"

And now, women can hear "You're going to prison."

Banning abortion leads to more illegal, and unsafe abortions.

"In countries where abortion is completely banned or permitted only to save the woman's life or preserve her physical health, only 1 in 4 abortions were safe; whereas, in countries where abortion is legal on broader grounds, nearly 9 in 10 abortions were done safely. Restricting access to abortions does not reduce the number of abortions."

Read it for yourself...

https://www.guttmacher.org/news-release/2017/worldwide-estimated-25-million-unsafe-abortions-occur-each-year

Daughters Having Daughters
by Allison Friske

I don't want to say,
but I have to say
that I don't want a daughter.
Not while she would strictly be
two breasts and an ass,
and no one would hear her voice.
The bell jar lifted, Sylvia said,
but to me it still hangs overhead.
My womb is eating itself,
crunching into a tight wad of paper
like the one thrown at me
telling me my tits are too small.
No. No daughter.
Lips as red as spring tulips,
their brightness fading as quickly
as a cheap blue jean.
The world is not made for daughters.
I dreamt of my daughter
taking the bell jar and slamming it
over the neck of her attacker,
his eyes bulging with the
force of woman.
No, the world is not made for daughters,
but perhaps I can make it one.

The Choice
by Lynne Schmidt

I wake up in the morning
with my dogs head on my stomach.
He usually cuddles with me
but he's never done this.
And when he makes eye contact
I know.
Allie says I'm being dumb.
Says maybe I'm just late.
Says I need to take a test.
But I've nearly failed every test I've taken,
and I don't want to gamble on this one.
I've never felt how five minutes
can feel like thirty underwater
I've never prayed so hard for
a black three letter word
Not
Not
Not
To
Not
Appear.
In the span of five minutes and one second
my body goes from being a mental health nightmare
to a prison.
My skin is a cell door
my breath is a lock

and I need to escape.
Allie tells me there is a key.
My friends tell me, there is a key,
that a doctor can save my life
and take this burden from me.
And I let them.

An abortion is nothing more than a medical procedure. Therefore, it's a basic human right.

Haunted
by Keana Águila Labra

i.
she was nineteen,
and he was gone,
she buried the tissues
ripe with blood as it
aged beneath an under-
standing sun,
the snake worn would forever hold
the name she would never wear,

just the night before
sprawled below,
as it pooled
pad after pad after
pad but the fear of
discovery kept her
from calling the
24-hour nurse,
is this not a red
alert, is this not
an emergency?

But in that moment,
she decided it would be
a much better fate
to die than
get caught.

ii.
she was twenty-one
and the next, when she swore
this would never happen again,
she remembers the doctor
asking if she would like
to keep the ultrasound.
Does he not know
how his words tear
more than skin?

iii.
She hesitated.

iv.
Does she regret?

v.
She is cursed with
guilt that she does not
deserve to bear.

This is for those who
were not as lucky,
whose limbs are strewn
atop doorways for only
the controlled to see
why must we always be
viewed as less than,

lesser than a collection
of cells with bars
of our own
undoing?

by Aries

you can whistle at me on the streets
tell me it's what i'm wearing
bullshit
my friend was once covered from head to toe
a man still followed her home
you can take me to bed
leave in the morning
tell me i'm no good anymore
i'm used
but who used me?
where have you been before me?
you can try to take away my strength
but you are afraid of me
and let me tell you one thing
you will never, ever
own my body
how dare you think
that you can even try
i am an ocean
and i will drown you
just you wait

-    *my body is mine.*

Stained
by Megan Gabler

The cement was stained from the streams of blood that flowed down
stolen from the ones protesting to protect our rights while we remained
silent,
hearing only the droplets dripping from open wounds
Smoke comforted our broken lungs as they screamed out against
injustice
We only watched in fear.
Fearing we must go into hiding
looking down at our hands and seeing as the streams poured their stain
onto us
darkness arriving as we hide knowing what dangers are ahead,
plucking away leeches with coat hangers
throwing ourselves down stairs for justice
not anymore, we have lost too much
we cannot go back to the past,
We must stand together to protect our own
wipe off the blood onto those who seek to harm us...
the living have voices and we must speak.

When Wait Cannot
by Sarah Lilius

I thought men were marching
in my body.
Scraping my internal organs
with signs.
Dumb words misspelled
like beotch and wumb.
Did I eat them
or did they just show up
one night when I was itchy
and sore?
There was no music
or light,
I didn't bleed but I
wanted to.
I thought men were trying
to leave my body
but really it's become
a hot spot.
Like a sports bar, driving range,
the couch.
Potato chips and whiskey
have formed a baby
in my uterus.
I doubt she'll survive
another night
but they'll try

to keep her alive with
their words, their torn signs.
I'm becoming a page,
I have paper-cuts.

They are my sons
running small
up and down
my body.
We wait for the men
to be gentlemen
and get out.
We'll burn their signs,
sleep in shifts,
just in case.

to violate
by Chloé Maria Winstanley

If Georgia & Alabama
freak you out for
fear of the
end
of
Roe v. Wade
I entirely understand.
when does it
not
seem like
women's rights
are under attack?

"...the implications of such legislation are clear: By prioritizing conservative ideology and those of the unborn over victims of sexual assault and other violent sexual crimes, the goal of such laws is not to protect lives, but to exert ultimate control over them. And for survivors of sexual abuse, who have already been subject to another person's horrific attempts to control and subjugate their bodies, such laws will have the effect of traumatizing them all over again."

~ Farah Diaz-Tello, senior counsel for If/When/How: Lawyering for Reproductive Justice.

Read it for yourself (and the sources too!)

https://www.rollingstone.com/culture/culture-features/alabama-abortion-law-rape-sexual-assault-punishment-835583/

Sunk
by Rachel Small

Pandemic of hands   trying to peel back skin. They dream
of uterus   a soft pink   like nurseries. Like flowers plucked,

morning dew still damp across fragile petals.   Love makes you
exposed.
Knots tubes into a noose, paints hands red.   Bad to fall backwards.

Their hands close doors.   They snap at bedsheets and expose
the crevices of your body. Movement is sacred.   You sit in the
shadow of a mountain

and wait. The horizon   is two long lines and you watch for their
slow arrival. Sun splits open.   You are blind. Eyes burning.

Your punishment is to walk   where you once floated.   Shed your
skin.
Salt burns your mouth   and you wonder if you are a body of
water.

Unmoving beneath   swollen moon. Debris under waves.   A body
tucked away. They travel across your water and turn you

filthy.

Hear Our Footsteps
by Kaitlyn Luckow

We are the daughters of
sashes and spells.
We are the sons of
lifting to reach equality.
Sermons of hate have
misted down on us,
but our feet march through
the fog
and we will make our voices heard.
We will write into history
that we matter.
That the blood of our veins
can overthrow the poison
in others.
That our cells that grow
within us
are ours and ours alone.
That our collective footsteps
can out-thunder the most
careless of storms.
We march on.

by Linda M. Crate

anchors of pain and rage
these bills aren't about babies,
but control;
and the fact some people
refuse to see that
makes my blood boil even hotter
than the bills themselves-
it's as if they seem to think of women
as nothing more than property,
that it is okay to enslave a person to their
needs;
their bloated sense of ego
or their emotions are allowed to dictate
laws-
i will always be pro-choice
because i believe it is no one's business
what you do with your life but your own
in the end we don't have to answer to other people in
the afterlife,
and so why all this judgment and this hate and this rage against
women?
we are magical, powerful, divine creatures and if it is a war they
truly want then we will sink their ships with all the
anchors of our pain and rage.

by Arys

sneakers against the cement
in the dead of night
i know that there are blood stains
in the space between my thighs

i sit down in the bathroom
when cement turns into brick
scrub away the blood
and try not to feel sick

a boy, humiliated
i'm still so confused
some say i'm girl who's been loved
rather than a boy who's been used

the night just gets harder
and i can't fall asleep
because my hands fall to my stomach
and my body's so weak

there was no protection
so it could very well be
i wanted to be sick again
had he left something inside me?

my body is not a woman's
despite what 'am i pregnant?' search results say
and the period trackers
that i download the next day

i do not buy a test
at the store down the street
because if i take one up to the counter,
i risk being seen

everything about it
it just feels so wrong
if this body's barely mine
than something else won't belong

about a week or two later
i'd never been so relieved to bleed
everything still felt wrong
but my body was handed back to me

and i've lived all my life
being told i'm not me
that i'm just confused
that who i am can't be

they call a man a woman
disregard his own mind
reduce me to my body
and still feel they're in the right

and now it's even scarier
to glance down at my skin
knowing the organs beneath
could take my freedom again

when they say that a fetus
is more important than me
they're not even calling me a woman
they're taking *everything*

they're not calling me human
they're calling me an incubator
my mind is irrelevant,
and that is so much worse

- *two cents from a man with a uterus*

There have already been 42 enacted restrictions on abortion in 2019.

(for reference, this book was published June 1st, 2019).

For updates, search this link:
https://www.guttmacher.org/state-policy

self-portrait in a target parking lot
by Courtney Felle

i am holding a pregnancy
       test when the man comes.

the man is big. scary. i do
       not see the details, only

impressions, snapshots of
       images. his hair, snarled

& tangled. his hands, callused
       & thick enough to choke

a throat red-raw. his mouth
       mottled, dripping, drilling

into my skull. baby, baby.
       come a little closer. i do

not feel my feet as i sprint
       into my car & click the lock
a split second before his fingers
       close around the door handle,

& i do not understand i am
       safe until i hear him screaming,

shit, you bitch, fists against
       the body's silver side, beating

& echoing as i make the drive

back to my school. the radio stays
silent. i am forgetting to fix
        the volume. i am sixteen. it takes me

another three years to say
        "attempted kidnapping," attempted

anything else. by then, i know
        my uterus flips & folds back

into itself, inverted, unlikely
                to ever hold a fetus. still,

shocked & crying when the
        abortion bills come for

my state, i imagine all the girls
        i could have been. when i tell

this story, the pregnancy test
        is always the first detail i include.

as if excusing why he chose
        me. as if he could have known.

as if to say, look how close
        this timeline came to every

thread in which a woman has
        to carry her kidnapper's kid,

a woman has to carry everything
        unwanted. i do not see the details,

only once a man almost assaulted
      me outside a supermarket & suddenly

i sat inside my school's ticking clock
      tower, trying to convince myself

the moment had ended. still,
      in my nightmares, my hands

are empty & the man keeps
      saying, shit, baby, bitch, come

closer. i am snarling, splitting
      throat open, trying to scream,

but my mouth has melted into
      the plastic bag, burrowed into

the pregnancy test's box. *i*
      promise, i can taste the words.

i am holding the handle. this is not my fault.

snap
by Emily May Portillo

it is ten a.m.
and i have not seen the sun in days.

the sky knows.
nature
is a mother, after all.
rage rumbles
deep in her womb
at the knowledge that ours
are no longer ours.

the man is rabid with power.
is followed eagerly
by froth-mouthed fools.
a pack of wild dogs
on a poisonous scent.

the storm is coming.
look up for the cracking open.
mothers
tear themselves apart
for the life they have given.
given.
did no one ever teach you?
gifts are not
to be stolen.

some war
is quiet.
some battlefields
are bloodless.
even so, we must fight.

we
whose bodies waltz with the moon,
will not drown in this tide.
have you been counting the beats
between the thunder
and the strike?

one mississippi
two alabama
three georgia
four ohio
five kentucky
six missouri
snap.

and the sky

explodes
into flame.

Sisterhood
by Ariel Moniz

Men
with their swords and guns,
with their laws and power
cannot touch it.
They are scared
of the forces that birthed the world,
scared of the true gods
scared of creation and its kind.
To them
we are vessels and sheaths,
waiting,
needing
to be filled.
They are wrong.
We are born
with all that we need
inside of us.
Armies, magic, pin drops of creation,
just enough to end all things.
Do we only live in servitude to avoid the call of destruction?

17
by Anonymous

I am seventeen
and if I ever get unwillingly pregnant,
I want it to be my right to make what I consider the best decision
for my body and my life.
I don't want anybody else to have the right
to make that decision for me.

I am seventeen
and I have big plans for the future.
I want to be somebody people listen to
and look up to.
I am seventeen
and I am still learning how to take care of myself.
And I am still getting to know
and trying to comprehend who I am.
I am seventeen
and there is a girl like me in Alabama,
in Ohio,
in Northern Ireland
and in many other places around the world.
The thought that
that girl might be forced to go through a pregnancy,
the thought that
she might be robbed of her right to become
whoever the hell she wants to be,
the thought that
she might have to put a hold on learning how to take care of herself
and instead will need to learn how to take care of another human life,
against her will,
sickens me,
frightens me,

makes me want to break her out of this prison
forged of outrageous laws,
take her into my arms
and tell her that it will be alright.
But it won't be.

I am seventeen
and if I ever get unwillingly pregnant,
I want it to be my right to make what I consider the best decision
for my body and my life.
I claim that right for myself
and I claim it for every person that is theoretically and practically
capable of giving birth.

the names they call us
by Jessica Minyard

they call us whores
when we get birth control
to tame the red flood
that stains countless panties,
pants, skirts, bed sheets
maybe we don't want to bleed
for three months straight
and a little pill is the answer
maybe we don't want to
wake up in a pool of blood
because, surprise!
maybe some of us
haven't even had sex yet
they call us whores
when we do decide to pop
that red cherry
because the tequila was too strong
they call us whores
when we get pregnant outside
of marriage and choose to carry
they call us lazy
when we can't afford
to feed or clothe or diaper our babies
they call us murderers
when we get pregnant outside
of marriage and choose to abort
they call us selfish
because don't you know
there are people desperate
to get pregnant and don't
you know the weight

of infertility should bear
down our shoulders

they call us failures
when the postpartum depression kicks in
because don't you know
a new baby is all sunshine and giggles
so why are you complaining
what will they call us
when there's nothing left
but parts
when all rights and dignity
and choices and humanity
have been stripped away
when we're nothing
but vessels for unborn
incubators for eggs
receptacles for cell clusters
have they picked a name for us yet?

reproductive rights are human rights.

The Unnamed Sea
by Tal Luxemburg

her grief was a feral thing;

unpredictable in the waning light
and carelessly handled at dusk.

in the unnamed season of her arrival,
she set out her womb to rot
in the swelter of her wasteland spring.

the decision came quickly in the evening;
came fiercely as revolution,
came plainly as birth right.

she had mothers to thank for this mettle,
and so cradled her relief easily
in a blanket of warm prerogative.

still, stigma caught in the back of her throat; caused a fever.
the root of it, like her grief,
an unrelenting beast buried deep inside her.

she hadn't anticipated the longing.
the unexpected tug of betrayal
echoed in an opinion not shaped with her potential.

still, it was a soft death, she reasoned, deserving of ritual;

she settled on two daffodils the colour of morning,
offered the wind each sun-soaked petal --

a pure love
preserved in non-becoming.

Bleedling
by Juliette Sebock

The room was so white that the sheer wisps
of curtain turned to evanescent opal
fluttering out the window
with each turn of the ceiling fan.
We must have thought it too white,
that we'd stain it red, maroon, crimson,
as if we sliced too swiftly through a blood orange,
brought you into, out of the world too quicky.
I don't think it left a stain,
but the room doesn't feel so white in retrospect.

Man Must Know Best
by Juliette Sebock

I should know better
than to read the comments
in a Facebook thread,
but I can't look away
because a man says
his wife is an OB/GYN
and would never turn away
a patient
for being too young
or because her
husband needs
to have his say.
All I can think is
I feel bad for his wife.
He seems to think
he's doing us a favour,
refuting the testimony
of this woman
when lives and rights
are at stake,
clearing the fake
news so we can focus
on being beautiful
dutiful
cis-het
wives.
Others in the comments
tell him that's great,
but his wife isn't
everyone's doctor.

Others say to shop around
(that's what we're bestat,
right?)
until we find someone
who'll concede
and it all reminds me
all too much
of a man coercing me
into having sex.
You know you want to
have kids someday.
You know you want to
settle down
with a nice boy
in a picket-fence
storybook house
and givea couple kids
his (now both of your)
last name.
You know you want to
fuck me.
Funnily enough,
no one bothers to ask
us what it is we want,
but pretend that
old white men
and those
who follow them
know what's in
our minds
the best.

notes to my future daughter
by Liza Rose

decades as decorations,
roses uprooted and replanted in
vases like prison cells of glass.
they wanted roses, but not their thorns.
they wanted women, but not their voices.
not much has changed, my dear.
*

the heart beats roughly eighty times a minute.
the thumping beneath your breast is an endless reminder
that you are not an object, not some soft-stemmed flower,
but that you are human and that you are worthy
of those rights.
(never forget that we have a heartbeat, too).
*

the fruit of a rose is called a rose hip.
if one were to try to take it away from the rose,
they would face its thorns.
the right of a woman is called human rights.
if one were to try to take them away from the woman,
they would face her voice.
thorns and all.
*

the prison cells of glass never truly went away,
no matter how many times women broke them,
they kept getting rebuilt in different forms
(i will teach you about the glass ceiling someday).
they have put the glass around us once more,
our ovaries on display for everyone to see
like items in store windows.
"look, but don't touch", a sign says,

but i can see my reflection in the glass.
i aim to break it, reclaim what is mine.
i aim to shatter it to dust so it can never
be rebuilt.
*

4 o'clock sharp. i look at the little
white pill in my palm and am so
thankful that it (at this time) is legal
and that i have it right here
in the palm of my hand.
i take it so that i can have you
at the right time, my future daughter,
so that i can be the best mother to you
that i can possibly be.
i want to give you the world.
i just hope that it is kinder to you
than it has proved to be
to the women of 2019.

What could be worse than an abortion?
by Danielle Burton

Imagine being born to a single mother in her teens who didn't want
you.
Imagine growing up in poverty because your mother wasn't quite
ready for you yet.
Imagine being bulled at school for your oversized uniform tearing at
the seams.
Imaging going to bed most nights hungry because your mother
couldn't afford to buy food
those weeks.
Imagine not being able to go to university like your friends because
your poor home life
caused you to fail school.
Imagine walking in on your mother crying because she felt like she
had failed you by not
being able to give you the very best.

Now imagine that this could have been avoided and you and your
mother could have had
the happy life you deserved together.
Imagine if this life was forced on the two of you by men you will
never meet; by men who are
much better off than you.
Imagine if your potential was robbed from you by people who believe
a heartbeat of a
potential being is of more value than actual human lives.
But you don't need to imagine it. This is not a dystopian poem, this is
a commentary of real
life. This is life that follows an abortion ban.

Barbed Wiring Casing
by Julianne Rosa

Woman,

There are many who have already predetermined who you are and
pretend that you,
someone they have never met, fit into a cookie cutter mold.

What they do not know is that they are pressing you into a barbed
wire casing by
assuming that you are nurturing, capable, willing, and desiring to
assume motherhood
at any given moment.

They do not know the intention of another's hand, how your money is
spent, who you
already support, the thoughts currently clouding your mind, your
fears, what you have
witnessed as a little girl, the complete and utter content of your
character, and the
history of unkindness flung upon you.

They fail to realize that every woman is vastly different, but we all
have one thing in
common: We have always been told to sit up straight with legs closed
and a mouth
partially open, to be unassuming and charismatic at the same time, to
speak when
spoken to but to also be the loudest voice in the room, to be a leader
but not bossy.

They tell us to be one of the boys. So, how come when we stand up
and approach the big

boys' table to reclaim a right that has never fully been guaranteed, we are met with even
more contradictions?

Wolves(Questions)
by Bettie Schade

Do the wolves not have enough sheep?
Not enough wool to sleep?
Not enough mutton to reap?
Why force us to bear your heaps?
Not enough bones to pick your teeth?
Are our gilded shackles not enough?
Our bells and bangles,
These acid brand bands on hobbled left hands,
Does ownership denied really challenge your pride?
Must you fill us with rocks so we must drown?
When all we want is our autonomy,
You take us, rape us, throw us aside,
Until we try to remove our trauma from inside,
There are more than enough resources to survive,
Why do you need control over our lives?
So again, I ask,
Do the wolves not have enough sheep?

It's not just women who need access to abortion.

non-binary people

trans-men

intersex people

gender non-conforming people

Need access to abortion too. Inclusivity is essential in the fight for reproductive rights.

Dear Alabama
by -Cpn-

Dear Alabama,

There are fifty states in our union, did you know that?

I only ask since you're ranked fiftieth amongst them all in education.

So, I figured I'd remind the world of that, using small words, in my alliteration.

In healthcare, you rank forty-sixth, which I guess is better than fifty; if you're comparing it.

Oh, and now to see where you lie, in economic opportunity, you stand at forty-five.

See, according to "U.S. News," and its ranking scores, your state is swimming,

like shit, in a musty bathroom stall.

Floating and waiting, intruding on the rest, with your obnoxious fuming fallacy,

at the worst you're almost best.

But even that isn't a feat you've learned to conquer yet.

You've managed to pass some bills that are as draconian as they get.

Since you're Alabama, you're probably too close-minded to see,

I'll tell you why your bill is wrong, and why you shouldn't let it be.

I'll start with the most obvious of it all,

you can't mix church values with congress; that's a fact, written-law.

Somehow, you have gotten over with leading states, bible in hand;

go around quoting anything you want, as "God's Plan."

So, your justification, that abortion is morally wrong,

is only based on your perception of what you think god would want.

Oh, but Alabama, that's not how it's supposed to be,

I guess no one has taught you that, most of your textbooks are old, as far back as 1933.

Mostly what you learn about is your pride in confederacy.

You've done no real research on what an abortion really is;

A medical procedure, it's not just used to "kill kids."

Sometimes a zygote doesn't turn into a fetus,

it merely stays inside, unsure of how to expel itself from the uterus.

Thus, this procedure helps in fact save a life,

of the person with the uterus with a decaying zygote inside.

Sometimes, bad people do bad things to others, even if they: say no, fight, and/or cry.

Unfortunately, anatomy doesn't know the difference between consensual and forced,

So it's not aware to expel what has been left inside.

Regardless of what you think you read in JOB 3-1-1-5.

You may not know, since you're Alabama so,

I'll explain what rape is; just so you know.

NO, RAPE IS NEVER CONSENSUAL!!

It's when one person, physically assaults another in a sexual way,

It happens to men too, and sometimes to kids of any age.

After this assault the body reacts as it would,

not knowing the heartache this person has withstood.

But her mind won't forget, it will surely cut her deep,

in her soul, the horrors, this victim will keep.

A few weeks later, they might turn up,

with an unwanted pregnancy.

Now, I don't advocate for abortion as birth control,

I won't encourage, it if there's options, but who am I to know.

I'm not God, so I'll never pretend

that all will be well for this victim in the end.

I bet if you educated yourself on contraceptives properly,

there'd be a whole lot of less unwanted pregnancies.

Maybe educate your resident on: rape, rape culture, and consent,

there'd be a lot less unplanned pregnancies then.

I'm not like Alabama, I read the part in the bible, that says that free will is in me.

So how could I ever take that away, from anyone, but especially

a little girl who has already been raped, made to see life differently.

The attacker took away her security, her trust in:

all people, herself, and humanity.

Now you force her to be reminded of that each day?

You don't have that right, even God would say,

In Peter 3-9 it is said and I quote

"he is patient with you, not wanting anyone to perish,

but everyone to come to repentance."

Alabama, let me tell you what that means,

Your god doesn't need you to be his jury or judge, you need to loosen the reigns.

If you read your bible right, only God decides who enters the gates.

But you may have interpreted the bible in the wrong way,

since you're uneducated, more so than the rest of the states;

I'd do well to reiterate, your views on god are not a template

for any law, at any time, in any of our "united" states.

Damn That Woman
by M. G. Hughes

They tell us they are there 100% yet
Claim we own only 75% of our body

They tell us their hands are open yet
Say we cannot open our own flesh

They tell us our legs and bones are
Everything that holds the world up yet

Dump a dumpster of paper over our heads
The inscription, I read, said

You must carry the seed of life
Or face legal humiliation

They say
They spat

They sway
They lie

Let a woman sow her own crop
But *Damn that woman* they say

If she raises her plow and
Proclaims *The handle belongs to me*

Dot
by Christina Rodriguez

On the anniversary of your expulsion / I visit the church for a mixture of penance / and breath, offering a streak of grief / over the station of flames of the Madonna Della Strada / The moment I enter, I see the crimson mouths of the idols / passion-tide veils to cover the sorrows of the mother I renounced / as a practice and a title / despite memorizing the grainy shape of a heartbeat I couldn't keep / out of desperation / I was raised out of desperation and my back still curves in habit / of being my mother's crutch / I refused to hit repeat while my axis was still trying to find / how to balance the damage / I refused to bear a circumstance instead of an altar / of love between bounds of flesh that have grown away from each other / I loved you but I worshiped fear and fear / told me the currency of a half-love with the seed that formed you / equals a death I didn't want to form in the flesh / better to drain you into crimson before you formed hands / that would touch my rib cage and pull me into forever / tethered to all the ways I would disappoint you / I loved you as I sat with pills pressed to the side of my cheeks / the choice of a prolonged ruin over the stirrups of a empty-handed standard procedure / I cried over porcelain blemished / with the eyes you'll never form / On the first anniversary I sat / pulling the skin on the back of my hands / the second, you met your grandfather in a zion I am / too numb to enter / and now I kneel in front of the covered face of la madre unbosoming / a grief I don't have permission to claim

If You're Not Angry, You're Not Paying Attention.
by Lauren Poole

i can tell you're really passionate about this.

your voice is condescending and light;

i guess you don't have to bear

the crushing weight of the trauma

of every grandmother along your family tree

buried in your throat.

i guess you haven't had to fell great oaks

in the garden of your mouth

to make enough paper to hold all of these stories,

for history to keep repeating itself,

for the same battle crimes in another woman's bed

mascara and blood like war paint all over the sheets

and suddenly this is all our fault

and the fight is kept out of the history books

so that the man can still be seen as the hero, the victor,

so he can still get into university, he has so much potential,

a champion swimmer, an athlete,

his body so used to claiming prizes he starts to see you as one, too.

when i tell this story

it falls from my tongue in tens of thousands of silenced voices;

some snarling,

some screaming,

some spitting,

all sexually violated.

all so used to your filthy hands

covering our mouths as you

thrust nightmares into women

that to you, are just bodies.

as children we feared monsters

under our beds, not realising that one day

the monsters would be in them.

not realising that one day

they'd repaint the walls of our

childhood bedrooms in the colour

of fear. that they'd close the door and go back

to the safety of the streets that have always been theirs,

that for us the door never closes,

they never fucking leave,

their hands crawl over us every night

like flies on a corpse

like a reminder that a part of me died

the night he used my body to feel a little more alive

as soon as i tell this story

everyone suddenly becomes a detective

and i am the suspect,

no stone left unturned, every second

of my story checked, more rubble left

in my room like my body once again needs

no search warrant.

but at the end of the day

you get to go home to your white picket fence

and your safe little dreamhouse

and i don't get to leave the crime scene.

i live in this room of nightmares

even when i am sleeping with angels

my demons are always there with us

and afterwards they torment me

drown my afterglow in darkness

with memories of the devil on top of me

don't tell me there is no need to be so angry

when he is busy writing the next chapter of his life

while part of me is still stuck in the one where

he took away my pen, my voice,

my bodily autonomy,

my fucking choice.

don't tell me there is no need to be so angry

when entire states in america are now taking away a woman's right to choose

when in alabama, doctors get more jail time for giving a rape victim an abortion than the

rapist does

and victims are forced to bear the child of the man who destroyed them

like a constant reminder of the worst night of their lives

when across the world, millions of women are being forced to defend their right to choose

what happens to their bodies

against the republicans smearing their laws all over them

when on the bus, creepy men stare like you're their property,

their eyes breaking and entering until you feel sick and empty

when in the UK, 1 in 5 women are sexually assaulted

when my male friends back home try to tell me that men and women are equal now

and that feminists have nothing to complain about

when in the developing world, 1 in 3 girls are forced into child
marriages

that strip away their futures

i am not another statistic

i am a force to be reckoned with

this is as much my story

as it is my mother's, her voice

always bold as a bonfire,

as it is my grandmother's,

her strength as blazing as

her abusive husband's van

the night she decided it was

his turn to taste flames

this story traces back generations

in every family. we have all had

dirty men's fingerprints branding our skin

with words like 'easy' or 'survivor' or 'victim'

like i've been reduced to something he was once in

don't tell me there's no need to be so angry

when i am tired of swallowing blades

and spitting out apologies

i am tired of pressing soft compassion

into filthy hands like i washed

their dirty laundry and handed it back

i am tired of trying to wash the stench

of my silenced 'no' out of my bedsheets

as if i don't sleep with this every night

i don't care if our abuse makes you lose your appetite

you tell me there's no need to be so angry

and i choke back the bones of thousands of victims

and say:

if you're not angry,

you're not paying attention.

Fatestrings
by Rebecca Kokitus

At times my mother will tell me she can sense the coming rain or snow in her body. I never understood it, but I always believed her. I started to feel the earth's pain inside me too, not long after my father's death.
On bitter-cold days I felt it, stark as an earring penetrating frostbitten cartilage, icy metal under my skin.

The earth was as tense as my body. I wanted to tell her that sometimes it feels good to open your body to the cold, to let yourself shiver, the warmth leaving your body in seismic waves.

The pain itself starts somewhere between my left buttock and thigh, then travels lower and lower along my sciatic nerve, like a dressmaker's soft yellow tape measuring a seam. The muscles in my left leg buzz like power lines. When I stand up from the toilet in the mornings, I feel lightning in my blood as I try to straighten out my spine. I curl and crumble like a slap bracelet around a wrist. I breathe in hisses through my teeth.

I silence the scream on the inhale.

...

Most things do not have only one catalyst. Most things do not make sense. I told myself a story about the root of my pain. The story went like this:

It was sometime in early May. I was home to visit my father. It would be the last time I'd ever see him.

He couldn't take the stairs anymore, so he used the tiny coat-closet-turned-bathroom in the corner of the kitchen. There was no light in there, only a toilet and some shelves, coated with dark dust, tainted by the coal stove. At some point between the toilet and the living room, where his hospital bed was, he decided he was too weak to walk, and laid down on the dull yellow linoleum.

He couldn't stand up on his own. After a few failed attempts to lift his body from the floor — he was so small then, yet I felt my back and hamstrings strain with the weight of him — I took off my flannel shirt and placed it beneath his balding head like a makeshift pillow.

His hair and beard were trimmed short then. I still remembered the first time I visited him in the hospital in February. How shocking it had been to see him so thin with a long gray beard. He had always been a round, hard man with a belly like a bowling ball, decorated with dark blue veins.

He looked up at me from the floor, his skin the same shade as the linoleum. We had the same golden Lithuanian skin. The same way mine had gone yellow as a smoker's teeth when I started starving my body in high school, his skin had also turned sallow. His eyes looked so green. He was looking right at me, but I don't think he saw me. His pupils were dilated. Come to think of it, he might've been strung out.

"I'm scared, Beck."

...

I told myself that this pain — always there, sometimes crippling, like grief — took root that night. I realize now that perhaps it didn't, but linking it to my father made me feel connected with him. His ghost nestled just below my left buttock like a cyst, like a tumor, shooting pain through me.

...

A new ghost nestled inside of me, deep in my guts. It didn't have a name. I never wanted to call it human. I called it "tadpole" because that's how it felt — like my womb was a bloated plastic bag from a pet store with some squirming thing inside.

At first it had been like getting butterflies, but more aimless and foreboding, like moths slamming against the single-bulb porch light.

Then there was pain, there was bile, there was the time I made my sister pull over outside of town so I could lean from her passenger side window and dry heave, a jagged and ugly sound in the small town silence.

I had taken the test already. My water had spurted out haphazardly, stung the dry skin on my hands. I'd glanced at it and seen that one line, that negative, that flatline, and buried it in the garbage. Now I can picture it seething there with its little blue crucifix.

The second time I took the test, there it was — that slow crisscross, like airplane contrails in a cloudless sky, crossing paths before they bloat and fade. Positive.

...

I couldn't get an appointment until two weeks after. Those two weeks dripped by like the end of June always does. I reveled in the times I forgot it was there, that little teeming thing — part me, part someone else, part fish with its eerie unblinking eyes and insatiable appetite.

The morning sickness came and went like a fickle lover, appearing unexpected and twisting up my insides like a dishrag, wrung out through my mouth. The vomit always came out clear and yellow like the inside of an egg.

I had never felt so alone and so reminded of the sin in my gut. I found a robin's egg on the sidewalk, cracked open. My stomach turned.

...

Like god, the body works in mysterious ways. My body had become a host to this parasite. I was exhausted. I lost weight. When my boyfriend ran his hands along my back and told me I was looking a little too thin, I reveled in the deliciousness of those words.

He scowled at the way my face would contort when we'd watch television, when I'd compare my body to every other body I saw: teenage girls in cropped shirts, women whose waists didn't fill their lovers' forearms. The ways my eating disorder manifested already exhausted him, but his annoyance seemed magnified during those weeks. He always made sure I ate and the child in me that I'd starved into silence basked in the cheeseburger and soft serve ice cream glory of summertime. It tasted like being a kid again.

The tadpole was curled up in me like some almost-frog, with useless little limbs and a comically long tongue that snapped out and caught calories like flies.

…

When the time came, the nurse asked me if I wanted to know anything about the ultrasound, but I couldn't bear to look at it. The infant in miniature like a Barbie baby. I had a pregnant Barbie doll when I was a child. Her smooth, tan belly collapsed in like a button, creating a crawl space for that terrifying plastic baby, and there was a round, new belly to snap into place with the baby rattling inside.

I imagined my 8 or 9-week old fetus looked like that. I imagined it had eyes that still had not grown eyelids, so it would be staring at me, still as a doll.

Tadpole, I reminded myself.

…

I left the clinic with instruction to swallow some pills, to push other pills up inside of me, wait for the poison to spread.

When the bleeding started, my entire torso felt ravaged, torn apart by something rabid. My womb was on fire. The pain was white hot and I knew this was death, secondhand. I laid down on the bathroom tiles.

This pain was unlike anything I'd ever felt—not like a bee sting, or a blow to the stomach—this was pain without an end in sight, horizonless. I was killing it, or it was killing me.

Vicodin stolen from my boyfriend's father's armoire lulled me to sleep.

...

I woke up to blood. When I undressed in the bathroom I stained the toilet seat and left drops on the tile. It came out steadily, reminding me of the way my mother would leave her sink running in the winter so the pipes wouldn't freeze. That thin, steady stream of water.

As I showered off the blood, a clump the size of a silver dollar fell out of me, slapped the pink porcelain and slipped down the drain. Just like that, it was gone. Out with the bath water.

It occurred to me then that it was the fourth of July.

...

The thought came to me from nowhere that my father—dead for one year and two months then—would be disappointed in me if he knew about the abortion. I lit a cigarette, felt the blood pooling beneath me like a shadow, like a trapdoor. I didn't apologize, not even silently.

Dad used to say you couldn't trust anything that bleeds for seven days and doesn't die. Now, I've bled for more.

...

At times, I feel defined by the pains I feel. At times, I try too hard to connect my physical and mental pains. The cutting of the fate string, the becoming of a muse. The dryrotted elastic of the sciatic nerve.

I am tension embodied. Perhaps I am feeling the storms building beyond my window. Perhaps my grief manifests itself physically each time I cannot cry at the thought of my father.

Or perhaps not.

this is how

revolutions

begin.

now, give a copy to your local legislators and let them know that this shit is ridiculous. let us govern our own bodies. and also – make sure you raise hell with your truth.

.

go to

www.wide-eyes-publishing.com

for more info, opportunities, and shenanigans.

www.ingramcontent.com/pod-product-compliance
Lightning Source LLC
Chambersburg PA
CBHW070819050426
42452CB00011B/2111